T0365614

# SNATCHED FROM MY MOTHER

THE TRUE LIFE STORY OF A KITTEN
SEPARATED FROM HER MOTHER
WHEN SHE WAS ONLY
ONE WEEK OLD.

by
Devinia Sookia

AuthorHouse™
1663 Liberty Drive
Bloomington, IN 47403
www.authorhouse.com
Phone: 833-262-8899

Because of the dynamic nature of the Internet, any web addresses or links contained in this book may have changed
since publication and may no longer be valid. The views expressed in this work are solely those of the author and do
not necessarily reflect the views of the publisher, and the publisher hereby disclaims any responsibility for them.

This book is printed on acid-free paper.

ISBN:      978-1-4259-1094-5 (sc)

Print information available on the last page.

Published by AuthorHouse  02/14/2025

authorHOUSE®

# DEDICATION

**T**his book is dedicated to the two men who have played a great role in my life ; first my father Gayadeen Gokulsing who was a very educated man with great love for people and animals alike . His dog "Bob " loved him so much that a few months after he passed away at the age of 57, "Bob "died as well. Secondly to my husband Bashir Sookia who is a great animal lover . He is always helping injured animals and birds .In Mauritius , he would always bury cats and dogs that have been driven over by cars and left to die on the road .Once he witnessed a very unusual incident .He saw ten cats surrounding the body of a dead cat as if to bid farewell to the dear departed one .

# FOREWORD

"Snatched from my mother " is a true story . It is the  life story of Titi  Pronounced (Chi Chi ) ;   a young cat of 2 years old born on a tropical and exotic island in the Indian Ocean  . Her life story is different from  many other  cats . Titi's life is full of intrigue , mystery , surprises , sadness and joy . This is a very unusual story in that Titi is the first one in her race to have emigrated to USA . Her story is full of emotions and will  bring tears to the eyes of readers .

# TABLE OF CONTENTS

# AFRICA

# CHAPTER 1

## Titi's Arrival

My name is Titi. I am a  yellow and white  long haired cat  and I am 4 years old. My head, tail  and back are yellow whereas my face and tummy are  white. I am slim with an oval face and big green eyes. I have a few beauty spots on my pink  lips  which are not visible.

I am  still young and well looked after. I am very agile and I can climb on any high furniture  as  I  have  a  well balanced diet. I  do not eat any fatty food. I am very fussy and like only one brand of  cat food  which is "Fancy Feast – Grilled". I used to like "whiskas" but I went off it. My favorites are grilled chicken, salmon and tuna.  I also have dry cat food which is full of vitamins  and  minerals  and very good for dental hygiene. My treats are peanut butter, chocolate, ice cream, olive oil and shrimps.

I like the shrimps steamed and not cooked otherwise. Now and then I like to have a little piece of steamed chicken breast or fried tuna fish chopped into tiny pieces as well as some boiled potato . I only like to drink fresh water. I do not like cow's milk. Cats are supposed to like catnip. I tasted catnip milk but I did not like it. However I like the dried catnip which my mum gets me from Petco. I like to nibble it. I also tasted soy milk and I did not like it. As far as cow milk is concerned, I have two reasons to dislike it. The first one is that I do not like its taste. The second reason is the main one. It reminds me of those horrible days and bad memories which I am about to tell you .

I was born at the end of November 2001 on the beautiful tropical island of Mauritius which is situated in the Indian Ocean, east of mainland Africa and Madagascar. I do not think many of you have heard about Mauritius. It is a tiny island surrounded by coral reefs and has lovely white beaches.

The sea is of a light green or blue color. The water is shallow and warm and you can take a swim all year round. It has a tropical climate.This means that the weather is always nice. Summers are hot and winters warm. Mauritius is multiracial and multicultural.

It is the island where the extinct bird known as the "Dodo" once lived. The first inhabitants of this island emigrated from Europe, Asia and Africa. The food is "Creole". Various tasty and exotic dishes can be found . Well, let me come back to my own story. I was telling you about my birth date. I cannot remember the exact date. I also cannot remember how many brothers and sisters I have.

All I can remember is that on a certain night in November 2001 when I was one week old, a big and wicked human being took me away from my mother . He placed me in a small carton box and took me out in the dark. From that day on I started hating human beings.That man left me on my own by the side of a street. Holes had been pierced in the box to enable me to breathe. I could peep through those holes . The box was so small that I could hardly move. It was very dark in there. I was feeling cold as temperatures drop during the night. I was very frightened. I was also worried and sad as I knew that I would never see my mother, brothers and sisters again . I tried to cry for help but it was useless. However I insisted until I became tired and weak and lost my voice. I could not meow any more. I was hungry as my mother had last breastfed me on Thursday at 6 o'clock in the evening and I was taken away at around 10 o'clock that night . I must have been in that box for a very long time and I must have passed away from fear or fallen asleep. When I came round, I could see daylight through the holes. I then realized that it was Friday.

I had already spent 12 hours in that box. I was tired and very sad. I could not understand why this person had removed me from my mother. I was innocent and had not harmed anyone.

All I wanted was to be with my mother, brothers and sisters. I could hear the voices of people and the noise of  car engines and I hoped that someone would rescue me. It was getting very hot  and I had difficulty breathing. Nothing happened for a long time. Then at around noon I heard someone whistling. Someone was near the box. I prayed that he would open the box and free me. My hopes vanished when the person  just kicked the box and then went away. I thought that my end was approaching and that no one would rescue me. Then when I thought all hopes were lost, I heard the whistling again. This time I realized that I had to do something to draw his attention. I picked up all my strength and uttered several little meows. The man opened the box and the expression on his face was one of shock and disbelief when he saw me

At last I could breathe fresh air. It was so bright outside that I had trouble opening my eyes. I also realized that I had been abandoned near the front gates of a big house. The man who opened the box seemed to live in that house. He took me inside and put me on the front patio. He then called for another human being to come and see what he had found. A woman came out of the house and seemed really surprised to see me. She asked the man several questions and seemed horrified to hear that I was left in a carton box on the street. The man was calling me nice names such as "my sweet little kitty ". He also told the woman that I was a little angel. I was desperate to use the bathroom but the patio was paved and there was no soil anywhere. I noticed a big flowerpot with soil in it . So I tried to jump in it but I was too little and weak. The man seemed to have read my intention. He took me in his arms and put me in the pot. After I did a little wee, I felt relieved. The woman went into the house and came back with two bowls,one with water and the other full of milk. I tasted the milk but hated it. It did not taste at all like my mother's milk.

I heard them say that I did not seem to like cow's milk. I still do not like cow's milk as it reminds me of the bad time in my life. Fresh water is my favorite drink. So I sipped the water instead.

The woman went back into the house and brought some soft creamy cheese in a little plate. She fed me with it.

These people seemed really nice and I did not understand why they were doing this for me. May be they were some angels and not human beings. The funny thing was that I thought they were angels while they called me little angel. After I was fed, I felt better and stronger. The man took me in his arms and brought me inside the house. It was big and seemed like a palace to me.

It  was very clean and smelt nice. It had a long corridor, several rooms which were fully carpeted  and a big living room with nice settees and  chairs. They found a big box and put a soft clean blanket in it.This  box was okay. It was not too high and I could see everything around me. The man went outside and came back with a carton box filled with soil. It was not a proper litter box but it had to do. The only problem was they put the litter box at the other end of the  corridor. When I  tried to reach it, I stumbled and fell. The woman noticed the effort  I had to make. She brought the litter box nearer to the box in which I was about to sleep. I was feeling really lonely and I was missing my mother. So I started crying and I cried myself to sleep. It was daylight when I was awakened by the sounds of birds. I was hungry, so I started meowing. The woman realized what was happening. So she woke up and fed me with soft creamy cheese and fresh water.The soft cheese was not too bad though it tasted nothing like my mother's milk.

I was feeling a little more secure and I knew that these two human beings were not like the one who had taken me away from my mother and treated me so badly. They were nice to me and I liked them. I thought of my mother who must have been worrying and pining for me. I missed my brothers and sisters. I  also knew that I would not see my mother again and that I had to put the past behind me. I was grateful that the woman was feeding me as I did not know how to eat yet. I was hardly able to suck my mother's milk when I was taken away. Later that day the woman went outside and came back with a plastic tray. She told the man that she was going to use it as a temporary litter box until they bought a good one. It was better than the  carton box which I had used so far. She transferred the soil into it. So that became my litter box for some time. I heard the two people discussing my fate. They talked about giving me away and mentioned the names of several people who might be interested in having a kitten .

# CHAPTER 2

## Titi Learns The Good News

I was hoping that they would keep me. I liked them and the big house. I was worried as I did not know what would happen to me. If they gave me to another human being, that person might not be so nice and might mistreat me. So I spent the whole day lying down in the box and waiting to hear about my fate and future. The woman kept an eye on me and made sure that I was comfortable. She seemed to guess what was going on in my little mind.  The man took me in his arms and  stroked me gently. I enjoyed the cuddle as it gave me comfort and reassurance .  I prayed to God to make them keep me .

After a few days I felt better and stronger, so I ventured out of the box and started walking. I went in the kitchen and sat on the kitchen floor. I tried to follow the woman wherever she went. Then I heard the good news. I learnt that these nice people  had decided to keep me and that from then on I was a member of their family. I was over the moon. I was so happy that I started jumping about. So I had found new parents. Though I had  a birth mother and loved her, I had found another mother who loved me as much as my birth one. I was very grateful and thanked God for that. My new parents decided to give me a name. As I had been found in a box on which the word "Rani " was printed and that word was a South Asian word which meant "Queen ", my parents gave me the name of the famous queen of Egypt which was "Nefertiti". According to my mother " Nefertiti" was an Egyptian queen who lived in Egypt centuries ago. She was the most beautiful woman that has ever lived on the face of this earth. She was also the first woman to wear mascara and eye makeup as she invented them. Her statue can be found in a German  museum and many tourists visit the museum just to look at the statue.

I felt very proud of my name and realized that my parents must have thought a lot of me to give me such a name. They must have thought I was very beautiful. As "Nefertiti" was too long, I was nicknamed "Tlti".

The day after my parents decided to adopt me, my father went out and bought a nice red collar, a red litter box and a big bag of litter. I was very happy as red is my favorite color. But I was not too satisfied with the litter as I was not used to it . I had been used to doing my business in the soil of the back garden when I was with my mother. It was ok to use soil in the box or the temporary tray. But using litter seemed a bit difficult. Nevertheless I started using it.

My mother had difficulty finding the right food for me. She bought some sort of cat food called "whiskas" but I could not eat it as its taste was horrible. It was nothing like the "whiskas" which is available here. She gave me cooked rice mashed with tinned sardines or tuna fish. I did not like it. I licked the bits of tuna or sardine and left the rice. One day my mum was frying fish .The smell gave me an appetite and I started to utter little meows.My mother immediately noticed my interest in the food. So she gave me some fried fish cut into little pieces. From then on she started frying fresh fish, chicken and chicken livers for me. On the same day my father put me in a wicker basket and took me to visit his friends. I did not like that basket but I had no choice. In the evening my parents were invited to dinner at a relative's place.They did not want to leave me behind, so I was placed on a blanket on the back seat of my father's van. My mother also took my litter tray,food and water. When we reached the relative's place, my father parked his van in the yard. Several children were playing there. As soon as my father took me out, they started shouting and wanted to touch me. My mother noticed my fear and asked my father to put me back in the van. I was nervous and disliked other human beings even though they were kids.

As I could hear my parents talking on the patio, I was not afraid. So I slept. I was really relieved when we came back home after a few hours.I was getting bigger and stronger everyday and I would follow my mother everywhere. I liked watching her do the washing up. I also enjoyed the sight of the water coming out of the tap. It seems that cats do not like water but I loved water. I liked to jump on the settees in the living room and on the

chairs in the kitchen. I would sit on one of the kitchen chairs and watch my mum cook or do house chores. I would sit on the broom when my mum swept.

When she did the  bed, I would hide under the sheet. My mum knew I was playful and enjoyed playing with me. She would let me hide under the bed sheet and then kiss my head.

She would play hide and seek with me. She would also sing to me in the evening. Sometimes she would  make me dance by holding my two forefeet when there was music on the radio or television. My parents did not like leaving me at home . So they tried to take me with them  in the car or van wherever possible. My parents took me to the beach. I had never seen the sea before and though I liked water, I did not like the sea. There was too much water for me.My dad put me on the white sandy beach. It was beautiful to look at but I did not like walking on it.So I jumped back on the car seat.

They took me to the beach twice and both times I refused to come out of the car. So they stopped taking me to the seaside. Instead we went round the island sightseeing. I enjoyed watching the sea, the beaches, casuarinas and coconut trees from the back seat of the van.

Once my mother took me to her sister's place. I liked it there as my mum's niece gave me some cheddar cheese.She was a nice person and seemed to like pets. Her little daughter kept stroking me and wanted to keep me for good. At first I did not feel like wandering on my own as there was a big dog outside. I stayed close to the living room where my mother was chatting. They had a lovely garden full of nice plants and flowers. It was such a nice and sunny day and the garden was so beautiful that I decided to play outside and watch the birds. When I was playing among the rose bushes a thorn pricked me in my back. It did not hurt much but when I got home, I had fever and my back was swollen. My mum only realized that there was something wrong with me when I refused to eat the pieces of chicken which she had fried for me.

# CHAPTER 3

## Titi''s First Visit To The Vet

My mum did her best to make me feel better. She gave some warm milk mixed with honey. Usually I cannot stand milk but as my mum put a little honey in it, it was not too bad. It soothed me and made me feel better. Now I have it when I am sick. My back did not hurt very much but I felt weak and did not have the energy to go outside to play . I missed chasing birds and butterflies or playing with roaches outside. My favorite playtime was in the early evening when roaches would come on the patio. I liked to play with them by preventing them from moving. I would place my front paw on them, then let them go. I would repeat this process until they stopped moving for good. My mother did not like me doing that and she would prevent me from doing that .

So as I had fever and my back hurt, I could not chase roaches or watch ants taking food to their moles. Though I did not feel too good, I did not want to worry my parents. I sat in the kitchen watching her and pretending that I was in perfect health. No matter how hard I tried, I could not eat and the food had a horrible taste. Finally I gave up trying to eat or pretending to be well. When I refused to eat, my mum realized I was not well. She told my father to take me to the vet as my back was swollen. I did not know what a vet was but I did not like it when my dad put me in the basket. When we reached the vet's office, there were many cats and dogs waiting to be seen. The vet took me out of the basket and gave me an injection. It hurt and I did not like the vet. When we came back home I was feeling better and my back was no longer swollen.I was happy until I heard my parents' talk about leaving Mauritius. They were discussing what to do with me. I understood that my parents did not live in Mauritius but had resided in London, United Kingdom for a very long time.

They had come to Mauritius for some time and had built a house in the town of Rose Hill. This is the town where I was born as well. It was now time for them to leave for the United States where they intended to reside permanently.That was the reason of their discussion about keeping me or not. Once more I started worrying. My mother told my father that they could not leave me behind and my father agreed. He said that they had to contact the necessary authorities and make travel arrangements for my trip. He also mentioned that he did not mind staying a little longer in Mauritius so that I could travel with them . I was happy again and knew that my parents would always keep me and would never abandon me as I was a member of the family.

My father started sending emails to the Ministry of Agriculture and Fisheries in United Kingdom to inquire about quarantine as they intended to go to USA through London. They had lived in London for a very long time and wanted to spend a few days there. In United Kingdom the quarantine rules were very strict. My parents could not go directly to USA as there was no direct flight from Mauritius to USA.They had to change plane somewhere in Europe. My father was trying all means possible so that we could leave soon. The Ministry of Agriculture and Fisheries in United Kingdom was taking a long time to reply.Meanwhile my mother called the American Embassy in Port Louis ; the capital of Mauritius to find out about pets entering USA. A lady told her to call back in two hours. When my mother called back, the lady had all the necessary information for her.She read the rules regarding entry of pets into USA on the phone and my mother made notes. Apparently there was no problem whatsoever for cats as far as the cat was healthy. My mother told the lady that she would get a health certificate from the vet in Mauritius to certify that I was healthy. My mother was very happy with the news.So my parents only had to wait for the reply from United Kingdom as to whether I could gain entry into that country without any problem .

# CHAPTER 4

## Titi is spayed

One day my mother was listening to the world news on television when she heard that the quarantine laws in England had been changed. Pet owners could bring their pets into the country if they had been placed with a microchip six months beforehand and if they had been vaccinated against rabies. So when my mother informed my father about this, he decided to see the Mauritian Government vet about the possibility of having this done in Mauritius.

My father was very upset when he came back from the government vet. First of all they did not have the facilities in Mauritius to place microchip. Secondly Mauritius was a rabies free island, so they did not have such vaccination. That same day my father's friend who lived in London sent an email informing my father that it would be very difficult for me to enter London if I did not comply with the British quarantine law.This meant that my parents would not be able to go through London. I felt sorry for them but could not do anything . My father was determined to take me to United states of America. He told my mum that he would postpone his travel until he was sure that I would be able to accompany him.Time was passing by and I was now three months old. My parents were hopeful about taking me with them as far as I had no problem entering USA. My father decided that it was best for me to be spayed while they were making travel arrangements. I did not know what that meant, so I waited to see what would happen to me.

The day before I was supposed to be spayed, my father told my mother to stop feeding me as from 8 o'clock that night. My mother seemed really worried, She

13

wanted to accompany us to the vet but my father told her that there was no need. She also told my father to call her as soon as he got to the vet's office.

The following morning I was placed in the basket and taken to the vet. As soon as I saw him, I knew that something bad would happen to me. When I refused to come out of the basket, my father decided that he would be the one to take me out. The vet put an injection in my neck and it hurt.Then I heard the vet tell my father to leave me behind and come back for me after five hours. I did not like being left behind but I was feeling groggy and went to sleep. I do not remember what happened.

When I woke up, I was lying on a white sheet which my mother had put on the big bed. The sheet was wet as I had vomited a lot of fluid. I do not know where all this water had come from but I was feeling cold. It seems like my mother had been checking on me every minute. So when she saw me shivering and noticed how weak I was, she told my father to call the vet as something was wrong . She also moved me from the bed and placed me on two big blankets on the floor. This seemed better as I was in pain and could only lie on one side. The vet reassured my parents that it was normal but to bring me back to him if I was still unwell the next morning. I hoped that I would be better the next day as I did not want to go back to him. I was thirsty and luckily my mum guessed so. She put a little honey in warm milk and fed me with a spoon. This tasted nice and I felt better.

After that I went back to sleep. The next morning I was still weak but I could move. The vet had shaved the left side of my tummy. I did not look a pretty sight. My father was not happy at all. He told my mum that if he knew the vet was going to do that to me, he would not have had me spayed. My mother said that she was sorry for me as I would not be able to have little "Titis". My father made her understand that it would be impossible to let me have kids when we were about to travel to a new country.

14

Then I understood what had happened to me. I started crying but  stopped as I understood that it had to be so as my parents did not have any choice. I also understood why that man had taken me away from my  mother and left me to die on the side of the street . I was a female and was going to give birth to kittens. Some people did not like having too many cats.My father told my mum to keep an eye on me in the coming days.

According to the vet I was not supposed to jump or climb on anything high during fifteen days. So all I could do was to lie on the kitchen floor and watched my mum do the housework. It was very hot but my mum closed all the doors and opened the windows just a little for fresh air. What I missed most was climbing on the plank which my father had built as a bridge for me to go onto the high wall and then into the neighboring woods. I  wanted to go the woods  to watch the birds and butterflies. I could not bear being inside all the time when there was so much  excitement outside. One day my mum forgot to close the kitchen door. I realized my luck and decided to venture outside. I was trying to jump on my so called bridge when my mother caught up with me and brought me back inside. From then on I had to sit by the kitchen door and watch through the glass. After fifteen days I felt stronger. I was looking forward to going outside again  when my father got hold of me and put me in the basket. I was worried as I knew that this meant going to the vet again. My mother tried to calm me down as she saw how upset I was.

She had some soothing words for me. My father told me that everything would be fine once the vet removed the stitches  and I would be able to run again.I did not understand what he meant but I trusted him.This time as well my father did not allow the vet to take me out of the basket. He did it himself and held me while the vet did something to my skin. It hurt but not as much as the injection did before. It was soon over and I was really happy when we got home.

My mum opened all doors and windows and I was allowed to go to my woods again. The fresh air was good. I could  chase the roaches and birds once more.

# CHAPTER 5

## Plane ticket for Titi

In the week that followed my father discovered a store which sold some sort of cat food imported from France. He got some for me to try. It had peas and carrots together with chicken or rabbit. Its taste was good. So from then on my father started getting me that nice French food.My father got in touch with the French and German Embassies to find out about pets entering in transit into France and Germany. Both told him that there was no problem.So he tried to book my ticket on an Air France plane as he decided to change plane in Paris, France.When the travel agency told him that I would not be able to travel with him in the passengers' cabin but would have to travel in the cargo section, my father refused to travel by Air France.

He was happy when the German plane Lufthansa announced that it would allow me as a cabin passenger. I could travel with my parents if they paid for my fare. My father was happy to do so. So everything was fine.The tickets were booked and we were about to leave in September 2002. Then something happened which really upset my mother and got my father worried. Some relative of my father who lives in Washington DC, USA phoned my father and informed him that pets were not allowed entry into USA. As it was my mother who had made all the necessary inquiries at the American Embassy, my father did not know what to do. So my mother gave him the contact name and phone number at the embassy so that he could call himself. When he did, the lady emailed him all the information on cats' entry into USA. There was no problem at all. My mother was not too happy as we were supposed to stay with that relative in USA for a few days before we settled in and got our own place. Anyway my father told my mother not to worry and that God would help us as always. That night my father prayed fervently before going to bed. I was beginning to feel sad, thinking that soon I would not be able to play in my woods again.

A few weeks before we were due to travel, my father's elder brother got sick. He was admitted into hospital with heart problems.

 He had to undergo serious heart surgery. My father felt it was his duty to postpone his departure  to give moral support to his brother, sister in law and niece.


So I put the thought of leaving my country away. I was happy that I would be able to watch the birds for some more time. The surgery went well and my uncle recovered. By that time it was nearly Christmas. My father's niece and sister in law asked my parents to stay and spend new year's eve with them. So  my father decided to leave Mauritius on January 11, 2003.  My birthday had come and gone. My parents  talked about the day they found me.

Mauritius is always affected by tropical storms from November to March. These storms are called cyclones and sometimes they cause severe damage to the sugar cane crops and to buildings.There were a few tropical storms in December 2002. During one of them I went outside though my mother tried to stop me. However I did not get far. I could hardly walk. The strong  winds  prevented me from walking and pushed me about. I came back wet and frightened. My mum dried me with my towel. She always used to keep a clean towel for me. Everyday when I returned from my woods at around 6 o'clock in the evening, she would brush me and then feed me. If I was covered in dirt, she would clean me with a sponge and soap.Then she would dry me up. After that I was not allowed to go out again.  So after I got soaked by the  cyclonic rain, I did not dare to venture out again.  I stayed inside till the storm calmed down. Then I discovered that the ground was soaked with water.There were fallen branches and leaves everywhere and no birds or butterflies could be seen.


One day my father brought two small kittens who were just like me, yellow and white.They were a few weeks old and had been left in some open space. My father kept them in a room where I could not see them. He wanted to keep them as well but it was impossible. He thought I did not know about their presence but I could smell

17

them. He got attached to them and this made me jealous. Then my father placed an ad in the local papers.Several  people phoned asking for only one kitten . My father refused to separate them. He wanted to have a home for both together. Then one day a very rich and important lady called and asked for both as a present to her husband. The husband was very fond of cats.So my father was relieved that the kittens got a good home though he was sad to part from them.

# CHAPTER 6
## Titi's Departure

In December all the school kids are on vacation.They spend all their time lighting firecrackers. I do not like firecrackers. On New Year's eve there was a barbecue at my uncle's place. Both my parents dressed in their best clothes and looked really nice. My mum fed me before leaving. She left the window which had iron bars on the inside open as usual so that I could get in and out.

As soon as they left, I decided to go for a walk into my woods as it was still early and daylight. I sat under a mango tree and relaxed. I fell asleep and was awakened by a loud noise. I thought the sky was falling on me. It was dark and I was frightened. Then I heard the neighbors shouting "Happy New Year ". I realized that it was midnight and that the noise was firecrackers.I had heard my parents say that at midnight thousands of firecrackers are lighted throughout the island at the same time. I could not move as I was paralyzed with fear. So I decided to stay put till daylight. I knew that my parents would worry when they got home and did not find me. But there was nothing I could do. Just after midnight I saw the light being switched on in our kitchen. Then I heard both my parents calling me. My father came over the wall into the woods with a flashlight but did not see me as I was in a hole under the tree. He went back to the house. All night I heard them calling. At 4 in the morning when it was dawn and the noise of the firecrackers stopped, I made my way to the house. As soon as I got through the kitchen window, my mum saw me. Both my parents were over the moon .

In the days that followed my parents were very busy sorting out things to take with them.It was not easy as my mum had loads of books and stuff. My father is the practical one. He wanted to travel light. So he gave most of his clothes and suits to the poor people in the area where we lived. My mother cleaned the whole place  as she wanted to leave the house as tidy as possible.

My father got carpenters to secure all the doors and windows of our house. He asked  the vet to give me something to calm me down during the trip. As we were leaving early in the morning, the vet could not do that. Instead my father's nephew who is a dental surgeon and a very nice young man gave  me an injection  to calm my nerves and  make me drowsy. In fact he drove us to the airport . Before we left for the airport, we went for breakfast at my uncle's house.  Many relatives  came to see  us off at Plaisance airport .  I was sad but as soon as I had the injection, I felt groggy and went to sleep. We were in the plane and I was in the basket on my father's lap when I woke up. I was a bit cold but my mum had put a nice warm blanket inside the basket. So  I went back to sleep until we reached Frankfurt in Germany. I did not have any problem with the airport officials.They let me in. At the airport  lobby we were welcomed by a nice young woman who gave my mum a lovely bouquet of flowers. She was my father's niece  and she lived in Frankfurt. She was accompanied by her husband and my father's sister who also lives there. We  stayed the night at that nice lady's house. She has some  beautiful kids who were happy to see me.They wanted to play with me. That young lady told my father that she loved cats. The next day her husband, herself and my father's sister accompanied us to the airport as we left for USA. The air hostesses on both Lufthansa planes were nice. They kept asking my father if I was ok. The  air pilots  were very caring and  came to see me once.

I was  worried when  I heard my   father tell my mother  that he hoped that the relative from Washington DC would be at the airport to pick us up.  We were supposed to stay with her and her husband . That was the same person who had phoned once before. I had a premonition that things were not going to be too good. My fears got worse when the pilot informed the passengers that weather was very bad in Washington DC. It had been snowing heavily and it  was freezing.  I did not know anything about snow. I wondered what it was like.  Would I be able to play in it. I had been used to a hot climate and did not like the cold.  What would this country be  like. Will  the people  be nice and do they like cats. Will my parents be happy here. All these questions began to pop in my head. I was still thinking of all this when it was time to get out of the plane.

# CHAPTER 7
## Titi's Arrival In USA

**W**e did not have any problem entering USA. The customs officer at Dulles airport in Washington DC asked if I was fine. Our problems started when my father realized that the relative who was supposed to pick us up was not there. He phoned that relative who pretended not to know that we were arriving. My father then phoned another relative ; a younger person. The first relative's husband and the younger one came to the airport several hours later. In the meantime I was hungry and thirsty. It was snowing heavily and very cold. I wanted to pee badly but I was inside that basket. My mother tried to keep me warm by keeping the basket close to her chest. When the relatives came, the younger one informed my father that no relative wanted a cat in their home. The other relative's husband seemed very angry. He did not even say hello to my mum and completely ignored her. He told my father that he would not be living in Washington DC for long and that my father should not have come to USA. He also said that we could not stay with him and his wife and that the cat was not welcome in his house. I was very hurt and I felt sorry for my parents.

My father was shocked but as he is a very determined person, he kept his calm. He decided to leave our luggage at the relatives' house and look for a motel. My mum was dying to go to the bathroom but she did not want to leave me outside in the snow to go to the relative's bathroom. My father asked the younger relative to take us to a motel. We found one which did not make any fuss about me staying there but a room was expensive. It cost $ 90 per day. Then my father had to go to the store to buy a litter tray, litter and food for me. It was dark and late. The teenage son of the younger relative accompanied my father. He was nice. He picked up a tray and a dish for me to eat my food. The weather was very bad. It was snowing heavily.

We stayed in that motel for one month, then moved to a small room in Virginia. The landlord was not a very nice man . He was supposed to be a religious man but he was mean. He made my parents pay $800 for a boiler room which he had converted into a small room. We stayed one month in that room. When we left he asked my father for $100 as I had supposedly damaged some old blinds on his window. This was not true.

# CHAPTER 8

## Titi Moves To California

It was very difficult for my father to look for a job as it was snowing everyday and we lived far from the city. We were also running out of pocket money. No relative was willing to help us and all this was because of me. My parents could not take it anymore. So they decided to move to North California. My father's relatives in Washington Dc were really awful and gave my dad and mum a hard time. They did not like me, treated me bad and were always horrible to me.Even on the day that my parents went to say good bye to them, they did not let my parents in because I was with them. They left my parents outside in the cold where they came to say goodbye. I was so cold that I peed on my mother. She had to take off her coat even though it was very cold.That day I was very sad. I had thought that everybody in America was going to be nice but I was mistaken. I wished we had never come to this country. Our flight to Oakland airport in California was a pleasant one. The air hostesses on North West Airlines were kind to me. At Dulles airport in Washington DC, my father bought a pet carrier and threw that ugly wicker basket away. I was pleased as the carrier was comfortable. When we arrived in California, I felt better.The weather was quite warm though it was not as hot as in Mauritius. I was glad that it did not snow like Washington DC and Virginia or Maryland where my father's relatives lived.

When we arrived in North California, we stayed with a friend in San Pablo for some time . This friend had a big garden with lots of plants and fruit trees . My father used to go out with his friend while my mother cooked nice food in the kitchen. I was allowed out to play outside . I loved running up and down the lawn. I would try to catch butterflies and birds. One day I went at the back of the house and into the garden next door. It was fun as the garden was full of overgrown grass.

Then I went into the house thinking it was the one where we lived. When a lady closed the kitchen door and drove away in her car, I realized that I had gone in the wrong house. I got worried and began to meow.

After a while I saw my father through the glass door in the kitchen. He was calling me and looking for me. I meowed as loud as I could. Fortunately he heard me. Both my parents came to the door of the house behind which I was standing. They did not know what to do. They were upset. My father called the police who told him that they could not do anything. My father went round the house, trying to find a way to go inside in order to get me out. He knew he did not have the right to do that. However he was prepared to do anything for me and later face the consequences. The house was very nice. It had new and thick beige carpets. If I was not scared and my parents were with me, I would have enjoyed taking a nap on the carpet in the living room. I would also have tried to catch the colorful fish in the big aquarium. But as I was on my own and realized that I was in some stranger's house, I was worried and could not wait to get out of there. I jumped on the window sill so that I could see my parents on the street. I did not know what was happening but I knew that my parents would not leave me in this house. I stayed on the window sill and felt safe as long as I could see them. Hours went past which seemed like a lifetime. Once or twice my dad came near the window. He told me in a reassuring voice to be patient. He told me that he was waiting for the lady of the house to come and that once she was back, I would be out. I was happy to hear him say so and I could not wait for that to happen.

I had gone inside the neighbor's house at 10 in the morning. It was 7 in the evening and the lady was not back. My parents had been standing on the street all day long waiting for her to come back. Finally she arrived at 8 o'clock. She was surprised to hear the story from my dad.She let my mum go inside her living room  to fetch me. I was on the window sill of  the living room.The lady explained that she left her kitchen door ajar and went to fetch something in her garden.Then she closed the door from outside and went to attend  a funeral  in another town . That is why she came back late. I was relieved when I became reunited with my parents.For some time my parents did not allow me to play  in the garden.

# CHAPTER 9

## Titi Is Lost In The Woods

My father bought an American car which was very spacious. He would take my mum and myself with him when he went for job interviews.He put my litter tray on one side at the back of the car and my food, dish and water bowl on the other. At first I was afraid to go in the car but with time I got used to it. People in other vehicles would wave at me. Kids were really happy to see me in the car. I would sit at the back and watch the scenery out of the window. The only time I did not like being in the car was at night.I did not like the flashlights of other vehicles.It seemed as if they were coming to get me. I was also really afraid of big trucks.

My father finally got a job and was about to start in a few days when something terrible happened. My parents had allowed me to play outside again. I was playing in the garden one day when a tabby cat joined me. From then on she came to play with me everyday. We would climb the pear and plum trees and play hide and seek. One Thursday my mum had a cold and was lying on the settee while my father went out for a coffee with his friend. My mother fell asleep and I followed the tabby to the big woods nearby . The tabby left me there and went away. He was an outdoor stray cat and was used to those woods He knew his way back to the nearby houses . These woods were different from those in Mauritius. They were dense and had no path or ways to get out . I was worried and frightened. There were all sorts of dangerous and wild animals which I learned later were called deer, coyote and snakes.The birds were not like the small colorful ones in my country. They were huge. There was no fresh water to drink except for muddy water in streams. Night came and this time I knew that my father would not be able to find me. He did not know where I was. I climbed up a tree and spent the night there.

On Friday I decided to find my way back but the woods was so dense that I did not know where to go. It seemed like I was going further from the place where I lived with my parents. At about two in the afternoon I heard my father's voice in the distance but could not see him. Then I could not hear him anymore. At 5 in the afternoon I heard both my parents' voice in the woods calling me.They were looking everywhere.Then they left. However they also left an echo of their voice in the woods. So I decided to follow the vibration of their voices. I was tired, hungry and thirsty and could hardly walk. I had not realized how big those woods were. But I was determined to find my way back to my parents. As night was approaching again, I decided to spend my second night on another tree just to be safe. At dawn I started walking. I walked many miles. I had to walk a lot before I could see a house. When I saw that house, I knew that I was on the right track My father drove by that house one day . Finally I arrived at the house where I lived at 1 o'clock in the afternoon on Saturday. My parents were not there and the house was closed. I had spent two days and two nights away from my parents. I was still very frightened. I decided to wait in the corner of the garage of another neighbor.This one was a family man, not the lonely lady whose house I had already visited once. I had seen the man and his kids when I used to play on the lawn. The man seemed to be a nice man and the small kids enjoyed watching me. His garage door was ajar and it seemed that he was not at home.

After 10 minutes the man came back home, closed his garage and went inside the house. I did not know what to do. Then I heard my father talking to my mother outside. I meowed loud and my father told my mum that he had heard me inside the garage. My mother lifted the flap of the letterbox in the garage and saw me.She started crying as she was so happy. Both my parents had not eaten or slept all the time I was missing. They informed the man that I was in his garage.The man let my parents in the garage and he was happy for them. I was very thirsty. So my mum gave me a bowl of nice fresh water as soon as we reached home. I felt better though I was exhausted.

28

My parents had done everything to look for me. They had looked in all the streets nearby, went from house to house asking people about me, given flyers, offered a substantial amount of money as reward, looked in shelters, placed posters in several stores and searched the woods. My father had walked every inch of the woods from 4 o'clock in the morning till night. My father's friend told him that he would never find me, to forget me and get on with what he had to do. He also mentioned that if I did come back, it would be a miracle. My mum was crying so much that she got sick. My parents did not give up. They looked for me and prayed hard.

A miracle did happen and the neighbors could not believe it . They all cheered and were happy at the outcome. They had given full moral support to my parents and they were happy for them. They were aware of the big job undertaken by my dad in looking for me and of his hard work. They also knew that I could have been killed by a coyote or I could have fallen in a deep hole. That night my parents said a special prayer and were thankful to God. I was also thankful to God for looking after me and reuniting me with my parents. I was so tired that I went into a sound sleep. For several days I had nightmares. I would dream that I was still in the woods and could not find my way back. Once I saw myself being eaten by a big wild dog which I believe they call a wolf. I woke up in sweats and was happy to find out that I was lying by my parents' bed and that everything was ok. In the days that followed I would be frightened whenever my father drove by the woods. My mum did not like it as well. She would try to cover my eyes or divert my attention. So my father stopped driving along that road. I tried to forget the incident in the woods but I was angry with myself for following that tabby cat. I can never forget my ordeal in the woods no matter how hard I try . I often hear my parents talking about it. I have heard my mum tell my dad that she does not like San Pablo because of what happened to me there.

# CHAPTER 10
## Conclusion

After this incident I was never allowed to go out. My father got a job in San Francisco and started working a few days later. After one month we moved to downtown San Francisco and we are still living there. I do not go outside but I do not mind. I can watch the pigeons from the windows of our downtown apartment and I have many toys to keep me busy. When we just moved to San Francisco, my dad used to drive my mum and myself to North Beach which is an area by the bay. He would park the car near the sea and we sat there watching the sea and the sea gulfs which are big birds.

I have seen cable and street cars with tourists and big stores in downtown San Francisco. My mum feeds pigeons from our apartment window everyday and I watch them. I also like watching television when they show commercials of cat food and cats who look like me. From the window of our apartment I can see other cats sitting on the window sill of their apartments. My neighbor is a white and yellow cat like me but he is fat and lazy. He seems to have problem moving about. I am happy as I get my favorite foods. My mum got me a special type of peanut butter which is low calorie and creamy. She also gives me soft cheese which is a lot creamier than the one I had in Mauritius. I still hate milk and can drink only water. She bought a special brush for me called pet groom. This brush runs with batteries but does not make any noise. It feels nice when my mum brushes me. She says I have to be brushed everyday to get rid of hairballs. If I swallow the hairballs while cleaning myself, I might get sick.

I still like water. I am always jumping in the bath tub. I like to drink fresh water from the bathroom tap. It tastes better than the water from the kitchen sink or bottled water. I like to put my front paw or right ear under the tap.

I still like to jump on chairs and settees.

I enjoy being fed from a spoon. My mother is very patient with me. She feeds me most of the time.

My favorite toys are two white fluffy rats which have the smell of catnip. My dad cuddles me everyday. My mum likes taking pictures of me. I receive emails from Petco. My parents have even used my name in their email address. My mum has bought a big bed for me. I do not hate human beings anymore. My parents are proof that there are decent people in this world. I have forgiven the man who harmed me in Mauritius and those who disliked me  and did not want me when I first came to USA. I am used to human beings now. There are good ones as well as bad ones in every country.

San Francisco is a nice and beautiful place. People in San Francisco are nice to pets. The plumber and engineers who come to our apartment say hello to me.Our neighbors like to watch me through the window. My mum tells me that the neighbors tell her how cute I am. Even the pest control man who comes to spray our apartment likes to talk to me. He likes my mum telling him about my live play toys ; how I like to play with roaches. He teases me and says that I am taking his job away from him if I kill the roaches by crushing them under my paw. When my parents go on vacation, they take me with them.

At SFO which is the airport for San Francisco, everybody makes a big fuss when I am checking in. Since we have moved to San Francisco, I have been on vacation twice. In November 2004, I went to Maryland with my parents. We traveled by South West Airline to Baltimore airport and stayed at Motel 6. Motel 6 allows pets to stay as guests. In June 2005 we went to the beautiful island of Galveston in Texas and we stayed at Holiday Inn.They also allow pets to stay as their guests .This was before hurricane Rita hit Galveston and surrounding areas of Beaumont and Houston. I hope that the hurricane did not cause too much damage to Galveston beach. We went by plane to Houston and from there my dad hired a car and we drove to Galveston Island. It was very hot and I saw the sea and nice beaches. It reminded me of Mauritius. I felt a bit homesick and I wondered what happened to my natural mother, brothers and sisters.

I have my own personal vet who is a very nice lady. My parents take me to her quite often for a check up. Before leaving Washington DC my parents took me to another nice lady vet in Virginia. She fitted me with a microchip, vaccinated me against rabies and gave me all my shots. She called me pumpkin. So now my parents can visit United Kingdom and take me with them. I can go anywhere without problem of entry. I hope that I can visit Mauritius one day and can still meet my natural mum. However it does not matter if I do not. I have great parents. I cannot stay without my mum for one day. My dad spoils me a lot. I am really grateful to both my parents. I still get frightened when I am on my own. I get nervous when I hear people shouting. I guess I will never forget the night when I was imprisoned in a tiny carton box with no air, no food and no water.

Though I was born in Mauritius, I consider myself as an American and USA is my country now. I often have nightmares and dream that someone has snatched me from my parents and is taking me away. But then I wake up and I am relieved to find that my parents are with me. I was unlucky when I was born but then my bad luck took a turn

for the best. I could not be happier with the way things are. My life has changed and is different from what it would have been if I had stayed with my natural mother or in my country of origin.

Well I should rather say that I am happy in America because I am with my parents.They are people who love me and care for me. I would be happy with them wherever they go. I hope that no kitten ever goes through what I went through in my early days. I also wish that people could be nicer to animals and treat them better. They do not realize that pets have feelings too and are just like human beings .

Recently I heard my dad telling my mum that we should take a trip to Mauritius in the near future. I am looking forward to that visit. I hope that my woods are still there. I also hope that men have not cut the mango and litchi trees under which I used to play. I know that I do not stand a chance to see my natural mother but I hope I do.

My dad is right when he says that I am the first Mauritian cat who has traveled miles and miles and who has emigrated to USA. My name should be in the Guinness Book of Records.

**<u>END</u>**

Printed in the United States
by Baker & Taylor Publisher Services

Printed in the United States
by Baker & Taylor Publisher Services